Don Paterson was born in Dundee in 1963. He works as a musician and editor.

Antonio Machado was born in Seville in 1875. He was the leading poet of the 'Generation of '98', a group of writers who, in the aftermath of the Spanish-American war, sought to redefine the idea of Spanishness. Their aim was to eradicate what they saw as a crippling parochialism in Spanish cultural life by importing a wide variety of international influences, both intellectual and artistic, while at the same time celebrating the distinct qualities of the Spanish landscape and people.

Machado spent much of his life as a teacher of French and Spanish literature in country schools. An outspoken supporter of the Republican cause in the civil war, Machado was forced to escape on foot to France in 1939. He died a month afterwards.

DON PATERSON

The Eyes

a version of
Antonio Machado

faber and faber
LONDON·NEW YORK

First published in 1999
by Faber and Faber Limited
3 Queen Square London WC1N 3AU

Published in the United States by Faber and Faber, Inc.,
a division of Farrar, Straus and Giroux, Inc., New York

Photoset by Wilmaset Ltd, Wirral
Printed in England by MPG Books Limited,
Victoria Square, Bodmin, Cornwall

These poems are versions from the poetry of Antonio Machado,
Poesias completas, published by Espasa Calpe, Madrid

Don Paterson is hereby identified as author of this
work in accordance with Section 77 of the Copyright,
Designs and Patents Act 1988

A CIP record for this book
is available from the British Library

ISBN 0–571–20055–9

Acknowledgements are due to the editors of the following publications,
where some of these poems first appeared: *New Writing 8*, *Metre*, *Verse*,
Landfall, *Thumbscrew* and *Waterstone's Guide to Scottish Books*.

2 4 6 8 10 9 7 5 3 1

for Tim Garland

Those who, by an inward cessation of all intellectual functioning, enter into an intimate union with ineffable light ... only speak of God by negation.

Denys l'Aréopagite, *Noms Divins*

... for instance, it gives an adequate explanation of the well-known fact that a room is less resonant when full of people than empty; for the soft material of the clothes of the audience is engaged in killing all vibrations that come into contact with it. The resonance of the room would not be diminished, however, if the audience were replaced by an equal number of undraped stone statues.

Percy C. Buck, *Acoustics for Musicians*

Contents

The Eyes

Advice

My advice? To watch, and wait for the tide to turn –
wait as the beached boat waits, without a thought
for either its own waiting, or departure.
As I put it so well myself: 'The patient triumph
since life is long, and art merely a toy.'

Well – okay – supposing life is short,
and the sea never touches your little boat –
just wait, and watch, and wait, for art is long;
whatever. To be quite honest with you,
none of this is terribly important.

Anacreontic

Yes – like Anacreon! –
I just want to sing,
to laugh, throw
all that sober,
reasonable advice
to the wind, then –
more than anything –
get completely tanked,
slaughtered, you know ...
ugly with the drink!
Between the beers,
this dubious shower
and that pure and undimmed
faith in my demise,
I'll somehow keep our
danse macabre
one step ahead of time ...
Cheers!

To Emiliano Barral

Plane by plane,
corner by corner,
your chisel struck upon me
holding my breath
in the frozen dawn
of this porphyry block,
or at least the man I now
want in my mirror:
the Spanish Buddha, in all
his idle grandeur!
The dumb, slaked mouth,
the ears set to the wall
of silence, and under
the bare slope of the brow,
eyes scooped from the rock –
from rock, that I might not see.

A Memory of Childhood

A winter afternoon. The sun
has gone in, and the class begun.
The students settle. Steady rain
lacerates the windowpane.

Dying bells; overhead
a faded poster showing Cain
fugitive, and Abel dead;
by his side, a crimson stain.

A scarecrow in a tattered cloak,
the ancient master slowly stands,
clears his throat, then starts to croak
from the rule-book in his hand.

The children rise at his command
then intone the dismal lesson:
A hundred hundreds make a thousand.
A thousand thousands make a million.

A winter afternoon. The sun
Has gone out, and the class begun.
The students study. Steady rain
lashes at the windowpane.

Chords

Perhaps, when we're half-asleep,
the same hand that sows the stars
trails across that galactic lyre ...
the dying wave reaching our lips
as two or three true words

Dream

I woke. Was it her breath or my own
that misted up the window of my dream?
My heart's all out of time ...
The black flame of the cypress in the orchard,
the lemon-blossom in the meadow ...
then a tear in the clouds,
the land brightening in its lantern
of sun and rain, the sudden rainbow;
then all of it, inverted, minuscule, in each speck
of rain in her black hair!
And I let it slip away again
like a soap-bubble in the wind ...

The Eyes

When his beloved died
he decided to grow old
and shut himself inside
the empty house, alone
with his memories of her
and the big sunny mirror
where she'd fixed her hair.
This great block of gold
he hoarded like a miser,
thinking here, at least,
he'd lock away the past,
keep one thing intact.

But around the first anniversary,
he began to wonder, to his horror,
about her eyes: *Were they brown or black,*
or grey? Green? Christ! I can't say ...

One Spring morning, something gave in him;
shouldering his twin grief like a cross,
he shut the front door, turned into the street
and had walked just ten yards, when, from a dark close,
he caught a flash of eyes. He lowered his hat-brim
and walked on ... *yes, they were like that; like that ...*

Profession of Faith

God is not the sea, but of its nature:
He scatters like the moonlight on the water
or appears on the horizon like a sail.
The sea is where He wakes, or sinks to dreams.
He made the sea, and like the clouds and storms
is born of it, over and over. Thus the Creator
finds himself revived by his own creature:
he thrives on the same spirit he exhales.

I'll make you, Lord, as you made me, restore
the soul you gifted me; in time, uncover
your name in my own. Let that pure source
that pours its empty heart out to us pour
through my heart too; and let the turbid river
of every heartless faith dry up for ever.

Gloss

Our lives are only rivers
that flow into the sea,
the sea, our end. Poetry.
Of all the makers I revere
Manrique speaks the most to me:
that delight in being alive,
in our just being here –
then time's hurried lesson
and the blind rush to the ocean;
how quick our dread of leaving
turns to joy when we arrive . . .
But that we might go back again!
Imagine the grieving . . .

Guadarrama

Is this you, Guadarrama, the old friend
I'd look for in the blue indifferent eye
of all those lonely evenings in Madrid?
Through your gorges, corries, ragged peaks,
a thousand suns, a thousand Guadarramas
are riding with me to the heart of you.

An Interrogation

I didn't know if it was a yellow lemon
you held in your hand, Guiomar,
or the spool where you'd wound
that single perfect day. (Do love's
derangements *unstring* the days,
cut them free from time?) I know
there was a smile on your lips . . .
What was it you were offering me?
Time come into fruit, stolen
from the grove? The unplayed time
of some stopped golden evening?
A sun you'd caught, asleep in the river?
The atom of the one true dawn
that will ignite the mountains?
The obol of your own absence?

Three Lyrics

Love invents the year, the day
the hour and its melody;
love invents the lover, even
the beloved. Nothing is proven
against love that the mouth you kissed
so hungrily did not exist.

∽

Lines for two sides of a fan:
  – *I desire you to forget* –
  – *I forget you to desire* –

∽

I'd paint you, alone
on the latter-day urn
of an old photograph,
or the mirror's false depths –
alive to your heart,
dead to your poet

Marginal Notes

Not the timeless marble
or the time-tied melody,
but the word in time.

∽

The spirit throws up its banks,
its mountains of ash and lead,
its Edenic groves ...

∽

All imagery
that isn't pulled from the river:
mere bijouterie.

∽

Prefer half-rhymes, or assonance:
ideally, the song says nothing
and would have no rhymes at all.

∽

Free verse?
You should flee it, rather,
if you find it so enslaving.

∽

Half-rhymes on verbs,
rhymes on time-words –
they're most precious.
Nouns and adjectives
are knots in a clear stream,
slow or slowing verbs
in that lyric grammar
where today is tomorrow,
yesterday, still

Meditation

Is my heart asleep?
Has the dream-hive
fallen still,
the wheel that drives
the mind's red mill
slowed and slowed
to a stop, each scoop
full of only shadow?

No, my heart's awake,
perfectly awake;
it watches the horizon
for the white sail, listens
along the shoreline
of the ancient silence

from New Songs

Beside the flowering mountain
the ocean's uproar.
Salt-grains in the honeycomb.

✍

By the black lagoon
sea-smell, jasmine:
Malaga dusk.

✍

Spring's come!
Where from?

✍

The Spring has come;
white hosannas
from the bramble-blossom!

✍

The white bees'
honeycomb:
full moon

✍

The fountain and the four
acacias flowering
in the little square.
The sun no longer burns our skin.
What an evening!
Sing, nightingale:
it's the same hour
in my soul

⌣

That Roman aqueduct,
we say round here,
and my love for you, girl –
there's steadfastness!

Nothing

So is this magic place to die with us?
I mean that world where memory still holds
the breath of your early life:
the white shadow of first love,
that voice that rose and fell
with your own heart, the hand
you'd dream of closing in your own ...
all those beloved burning things
that dawned on us,
lit up the inner sky?
Is this whole world to vanish when we die,
this life that we made new in our own fashion?
Have the crucibles and anvils of the soul
been working for the dust and for the wind?

from One Day's Poem

So here he is,
your man, the Modern Languages Teacher
(late occupant of the ghost-chair,
ahem, of *gaya ciencia*,
the nightingale's apprentice)
in a dark sprawl somewhere between
Andalusia and La Mancha.
Winter. A fire lit.
Outside a fine rain
swithers between mist and sleet.
Imagining myself a farmer,
I think of the good Lord astride
the tilled fields, tapping the side
of his great riddle, keeping up
the steady murmur
over the parched crops,
over the olive-groves and vineyards.
They've prayed hard
and now they can sing their hosannas:
those with new-sown wheat,
those who'll pick
the fattened olives,
those, who in their whole lives
aspire to no more luck
than enough to eat;
those who now, as ever,
put all their little silver
on one turn of the wheel,
the terrible wheel of the seasons.

In my room, brilliant
with the pearl-light
of winter, strained
through cloud and glass and rain,
I dream and meditate.
The clock
glitters on the wall,
its ticktock
drifting in and out
of my head. *Ticktock, ticktock*,
there; now I hear it.
Ticktock, ticktock, the dead click
of its mechanical heart ...
In these towns, one fights –
oh for a second's respite! –
with those bleak hiccups
from the clock's blank face
that count out time as emptiness,
like a tailor taking his measuring-tape
to yard on yard of space.
But your hour, is it *the* hour?
Your time, friend, is it ours?
(*ticktock, ticktock*) On a day
(*ticktock*) you would say had passed
death took away
the thing that I held dearest.

Bells in the distance.

The rain drums harder
on the windowpanes.
A farmer again,
I go back to my fields of grain ...

... It's getting darker:
I watch the filament
redden and glow;
I'd get more light from a match
or the moonshine.
God knows where my glasses went –
(if one had to define
the pointless search!)
amongst these reviews, old papers ...
who'd find anything?
... Aha. Here we go.
New books.
I open one by Unamuno –
the pride and joy
of our Spanish revival –
no, *renaissance*, to hell
with it ... This country dominie
has always carried the torch for you,
Rector of Salamanca.
This philosophy of yours
you call dilettantish,
just a balancing act –
Don Miguel, it's mine too.
It's water from the true source,
a downpour, then a burn, a cataract,
always alive, always fugitive ... it's poetry,
a real thing of the heart.

But can we really build on it?
There's no foundation
in the spirit or the wind –
no anchorage, no anchor;
only the work –

our rowing or sailing
towards the shoreless ocean ...

Henri Bergson: *The Immediate
Data of Consciousness*. Looks
like another of these French tricks ...
This Bergson is a rogue,
Master Unamuno, true?
I'd sooner take that boy
from Königsberg
and his – how'd you put it –
salto inmortal ...
that devilish jew
worked out free will
within his own four walls.
It's okay, I guess – every scholar
with his headache, every lunatic
wrestling with his ...

I suppose it matters
in this short, troublesome affair
whether we're slaves or free;
but, if we're all bound for the sea,
it's all the same in the end.
God, these country backwaters!
All our idle notes and glosses
soon show up for what they are:
the yawns of Solomon ...
no, more like Ecclesiastes:
a solitude of solitudes,
vanity of vanities ...

... The rain's slacking off.
Umbrella, hat, gaberdine, galoshes ...
Right. I'm out of here.

Paradoxes

Just as the lover's sky is bluest
the poet's muse is his alone;
the dead verse and its readership
have lives and muses of their own.
The poem we think we have *made up*
may still turn out to be our truest.

Only in our sorrows do we live
within the heart of consciousness, the lie.
Meeting his master crying in the road,
a student took Solon to task: 'But why,
your son long in the ground, do you still grieve
if, as you say, man's tears avail him nothing?'
'Young friend,' said Solon, lifting his old head,
'I weep *because* my tears avail me nothing.'

Poem

I want neither glory
nor that, in the memory
of men, my songs survive;
but still ... those subtle worlds,
those weightless mother-of-pearl
soap-bubbles of mine ... I just love
the way they set off, all tarted up
in sunburst and scarlet, hover
low in the blue sky, quiver,
then suddenly pop

Poetry

In the same way that the mindless diamond keeps
one spark of the planet's early fires
trapped forever in its net of ice,
it's not love's later heat that poetry holds,
but the atom of the love that drew it forth
from the silence: so if the bright coal of his love
begins to smoulder, the poet hears his voice
suddenly forced, like a bar-room singer's – boastful
with his own huge feeling, or drowned by violins;
but if it yields a steadier light, he knows
the pure verse, when it finally comes, will sound
like a mountain spring, anonymous and serene.

Beneath the blue oblivious sky, the water
sings of nothing, not your name, not mine.

Promethean

The traveller is the aggregate of the road.
In a walled garden beside the ocean's ear
he carries his whole journey on his coat –
the hoarfrost and the coffee-smell, the dry heat
of the hay, the dog-rose, the bitter woodsmoke.
The long day's veteran, he puts a brake
on all sentiment, and waits for the slow word
to surface in his mind, as if for air.

This was my dream – and then I dreamt that time,
that quiet assassin drawing us through the days
towards our end, was just another dream ...
And at that, I saw the gentle traveller lift
his palm to the low sun, and make a gift
of it: the Name, the Word, the ashless blaze.

Proverbs

You see an eye
because it sees you

～

Seek him in the mirror,
your fellow traveller.

～

Your Narcissus
begins to fade
as he *becomes* the glass.

～

Always today, always

～

The Sun in Aries; my window
open to the cold air ... listen:
the dusk has awoken the river

～

And deeper down ... listen:
the water in the living rock
of my own heart

❧

A surprise – the smell
of ripe lemons
in the rose-leaves ...

❧

Now Spring has arrived,
don't chew on the wax –
get out of the hive!

❧

In my solitude
I have seen things
that are not true.

❧

Water, thirst, sun, shadow – they're all good things.
There's a honey from the flowerless fields
as well as from the rosemary-flowers.

❧

At the side of the road
there's a stone fountain
and a small earthen jug –
glug – that no one steals.

～

So ... what's meant
by the spring, the jug
and the water?

～

... but I've seen men drink
from ditches;
ah, the caprices
of the parched mind ...

～

Singers: best
to leave the cheering
to the rest.

～

Singers, wake up:
the echoes have stopped

～

It's not the true
I the poet's after:
it's the *you*

～

... But that *you* in my song
doesn't mean you, pal;
no – that's me.

～

What the wise
forget to say
is that today's
always today

～

Christ taught: love your brother
as yourself, but don't forget –
you're one thing, he's another.

～

He spoke another truth:
find the you that isn't yours
and *can't* be.

～

[33]

So many lies
from the man
who can't fantasise

～

You told a half-truth?
Now you'll be twice a liar
if you tell the other half.

～

All things in good time –
like the river, the lover,
the cup must be full
before it runs over

～

After the life and the dream
comes what matters most:
the awakening

～

His thin voice trembles when he sings;
he thinks they don't know art –
it's not his song they hiss at, though:
they're hissing at his heart

～

Have you heard the latest?
cogito ergo non sum.
In your dreams . . .

~

Two gypsies:
'Where're you taking us?'
'A detour on the shortcut.'

~

Hey – let's divide the work, so
the bad guys dip the arrows,
the good guys flex the bow . . .

~

To keep the wind working,
he sewed the dead leaves back again

~

Bees, singers, remember:
it's not the honey you're
sipping at – it's the *flower.*

~

Light your poem from two angles:
one for the straight reading,
one for the sidelong

≈

Not the sunrise
but the waking bell

≈

Among figs I am soft as a fig,
among rocks, hard as rock;
in other words ... useless.

≈

Your truth? No, *the* truth.
Come on, we'll look for it.
Yours ... please, keep it.

≈

Guadalquivir!
I've seen you in Cazorla,
clear water bubbling
under a green pine;
and today, dying in Sanlúcar.
As you slow with salt and mud
and the sea draws near,
do you thrill with the blood
of your first Spring
as I do mine?

✍

Take an old man's word:
not his advice

✍

But Art? ... pure play,
which is to say, pure life,
which is to say, pure fire.
We'll see it, one day.

Road

Traveller, your footprints are
the only path, the only track:
wayfarer, there is no way,
there is no map or Northern star,
just a blank page and a starless dark;
and should you turn round to admire
the distance that you've made today
the road will billow into dust.
No way on and no way back,
there is no way, my comrade: trust
your own quick step, the end's delay,
the vanished trail of your own wake,
wayfarer, sea-walker, Christ.

The Reply

Down the windswept galleries
and bare arcades of the soul,
the shadows of the days
slide like gunsmoke ...
The drunken chorus echoes away
as surely as our cloistered praises ...
History ushers through the bridal dawns,
each with her blue train of dying stars ...
And today – is some new ark
trailing its wake of diamonds
over the swollen belly of the globe
or has the old keel run aground?
Is the tired world sinking in its sin
or rising through it, saved again?
Again? Only God can say ...

Just then, a thunderblast from the clouds
stopped our lonely poet in mid-line.
He touched his left ear and found blood.
Looking down, he saw the empty plain
fill with the shadows of great armies;
and heard, in the clamour of the ocean,
the sick exhaustion of a thousand slaves;
and beyond the sunless forests in the north
found the NIHIL scorched and smoking
on the blank rock. Beyond that
there was only the road, the thin road,
winding over the far mountain.

Revenant

This must be her house, then;
its charred, wormy frame
tottering like a skeleton
on the mound of its own rubble.

The moon ships down a light
I take for silver on the windows.
Miserable in my bad coat
I head back down the street.

Ricochet

On an evening as empty and vast as my boredom,
under the brandished spear of the summer,
I watched as a thousand black shadows grew upright
over the plain, as if stones had been raised
above every low barrow and mound, every molehill:

it felt like my own half-lit, miserable dream
had come alive, that the sun's livid mirror
repeated my every black thought to infinity.
I struck the baked ground with my heel, and it rang
through the whole bloody west like a gunshot.

Seeing

On those bright, sad days at the seasons' edge
– if the light or the tears haven't closed your eyes for you –
you'll truly know yourself if you can find,
deep within in the gutted memory,
beyond the turn of some ruined corridor,
the picture-gallery of blacknesses
that were your earliest dreams, and one by one
stare them back to perspicacity.
Among the mind's gifts, this is cardinal.

Siesta

Now that, halfway home, the fire-fish swims
between the cypress and that highest blue
into which the blind boy lately flew
in his white stone, and with the ivory poem
of the cicada ringing hollow in the elm,
let us praise the Lord –
the black print of his good hand! – who has declared
this silence in the pandemonium.

To the God of absence and of aftermath,
of the anchor in the sea, the brimming sea ...
whose truant omnipresence sets us free
from this world, and firmly on the one true path,
with our cup of shadows overflowing, with
our hearts uplifted, heavy and half-starved,
let us honour Him who made the Void, and carved
these few words from the thin air of our faith.

Sigh

Again
my heart
creaks
on its hinge
and with a long
sigh
opens on
the arcade
of my short
history
where
the orange
and acacia
are flowering
in the courtyard
and the fountain
sings
then speaks
its love-song
to no one

Sleep

Dreams set down a web of paths
over the dark land; a garden
of grey lilies, opening in silence;
a labyrinth that will carry your cry
for hours, and a well that won't return it;
tiny fanes to the beggared gods,
padlocked vaults, a lunatic staircase
that coils through the trees ...

Little marionettes click past
with the known faces of the dead.
And now, where the path suddenly flowers
and turns, something dawn-cloaked,
chimerical, escapes into the distance ...

Song

Sing it with me now: we know as little as the stone;
we come from a forgotten sea, and go to an unknown;
between these two, there stands another, graver mystery.
Three chests that hold God-only-knows, all locked by one lost ke
The light throws no light on itself, nor all our brilliant talk.
What is it the *word* says to us? The water in the rock?

3 O'clock

The plaza and the blazing orange-trees,
  laden with fat suns.

Then chaos from the little school –
  the stiff air suddenly filled
    with shrieks and yells –

that wild joy
  in the corners of the dead cities!

And something we were yesterday
  that we discover still alive,
    like a river's pulse
      just below the ancient streets ...

The Time

Midnight: twelve dull blows
of the shovel on the earth ...
I shook out from my dream
thinking, *my hour's come ...*

But then the silence answered me:
Quiet, now: there's nothing to fear.
You'll never see the final drop
that trembles in the waterclock,

but sleep for hours, years, in this empty cove
with the white sun rolling red across your eyes;
and then one day – not now, not here – wake up
to find the boat tied to the other shore.

Tryst

One day, we sit ourselves down by the road.
Our one concern, now we are a matter of time,
is to perfect the desperate attitude
of our long waiting; but she will not fail to come.

The Visit

One night last summer
I was lying in bed, unable to sleep,
the balcony and front door
thrown open to the hot night,
when Death walked into the house.

He swept up to her bedside
without so much as a glance
in my direction, and set about
snapping something very fine
between his long, delicate fingers.

What are you doing? I hissed –
but soundlessly, as though on rails,
he slid backwards through the room again.
My little one frowned but only
in her own dream, and I lay

wondering what the threads were
that he'd broken so carefully.
And as I watched her breast rise and fall
my heart grew strangely heavy,
then heavy again with the knowledge.

The Waterwheel

The evening is falling,
dusty and sad;
the millstream still mutters
its little work-song
in the slats and the scoops
of the slowing wheel;
the mule's drifting off
–poor old mule! –
as the shadows grow long
in the sound of the water.

What divine poet
blindfolded you,
my wretched old pal,
and tied the perpetual
wheel to the water's
mindless soliloquy,
I can't say, but know this:
his was a heart
ripened in darkness
and slowed with knowledge.

Two Winter Poems

Against the blue, a ribbon

                    of black choughs,

   screeching and flapping,

       come to rest
on a stiff, leafless tree.
   One by one, the grave birds
     set themselves down
       in the stillness and silence;
       cold black notes
       on February's staff.

                ～

Like the rainbow in white light,
the same light that fills up
my empty stereoscope,
Pythagoras's lyre
sings on through the hush.
I sit, my eyes shut tight
and stinging with the ash
of Heraclitean fire.
The world, in this bright second,
is empty, voiceless, blind.

The Work

My heart was where a hundred dusty roads
crossed and then ran on; or it was a station
full of hopeful travellers, though not one
had either lodgings or a real appointment.
Whatever it was – my heart, within a day,
was scattered on a hundred winds, and sped
through canyons, deserts, river-plains and valleys
to dark ports, sea-lanes, unmapped continents.

But now, like a swarm returning to the hive
at that purple hour when all the crows go hoarse
and sail off to the crags and the black eaves,
my heart turns to its melancholy work
with honey gathered from a hundred flowers
and the hundred sorrows of the gathering dark.

To the Great Zero

When the *I Am That I Am* made nothingness
and, as He deserved, went back to sleep –
day had night, and man companionship
in woman's absence. He was bored to death.
Fiat Umbra! And on that godless Sabbath
man laid his first thought: the cosmic egg,
chill and pale and filled with weightless fog,
hovered like a face before his face.

The zero integral, that empty sphere:
only when our heads are in the air
is it ours. So now the beast is on his feet
and the miracle of non-being complete –
let's rise, and make this toast: a border-song
to forgetting, amnesty, oblivion.

Afterword

There are several Antonio Machados, but I've only tried to
write the poem Machado is for me, one about God and
love and memory; to that extent this book is really one
poem. There are few of the Spanish georgics, and there's
little of the more surreal writing here; it was never my in-
tention that all or any of the various poets calling them-
selves Antonio Machado be 'fairly' represented – though
most other selections of his work, in omitting, for example,
the writing of his heteronymous philosophers Abel Martín
and Juan de Mareina, arguably present just as misleading a
picture.

Reading a poet through the lens of his or her biography
is a dubious practice at the best of times; in Machado's case
it is a grave error, not least because Machado himself
would have abhorred this kind of reading – a fact that
becomes clear from the most cursory acquaintance with his
work. I can think of no writer so obsessed with the suppres-
sion of his own ego, and he would have been disappointed
in any reader who sought to 'explain' a poem in terms of a
geographic or psychological provenance. For that reason
the reader will have to make do with the biographical infor-
mation inside the cover; for a more complete picture, and a
brilliant critical overview of the original work, they should
turn to Alan Trueblood's *Antonio Machado: Selected
Poems*.

These poems are versions, not translations. A reader
looking for an accurate translation of Antonio Machodo's
words, then, should stop here and go out and buy another
book – again, probably Trueblood's, which although it isn't

poetry, at least gives a more reliable reflection of the surface life of Machado's verse. Poems, though, are considerably more than the agglomerated meaning of their words, and in writing these versions I initially tried to be true to a poem's argument and to its vision – if not its individual images – and to the poetic conventions of the language in which I was writing, rather than to its lexis. (Being true to a 'spirit' rather than a literal meaning is, I acknowledge, a hopelessly subjective business – and one more reason to plead with the reader to forget the relation in which these poems stand to the originals, if he or she knows them.) This quickly became the more familiar project of trying to make a musical and argumentative unity of the material at hand, and this consideration, in overriding all others, led to mangling, shifts of emphasis, omission, deliberate mistranslation, the conflation of different poems, the insertion of whole new lines and on a few occasions the writing of entirely new poems. In the end it became about nothing more than a commitment to a *process* – what Machado everywhere refers to as 'the road'. Perhaps it is the principal lesson Machado has to teach us: our faith should be directed only towards the unalloyed fact of the present moment, and therefore only towards means, and not to beginnings or ends; I interpreted it as a direction to cut my sentimental ties with the 'originals' altogether.

All this may need considerable justification in the eyes of some readers. It should surely, by now, be axiomatic that poetry cannot be translated in a way that will preserve anything of the flavour of the original. Poems are custom-built churches in which the poem's own voice – or the poet's, if he or she mistakenly conflates the two – can sing freely; but one so specifically calibrated to maximise the resonant *potential* of that voice, that another voice, upon entering the same space, is almost guaranteed to fall flat. Preserving either the rough sense of the words, or the crudest aspects of the original poem's architecture – the rhyme scheme, metre and stanza – in the hope that it will capture something of the first voice is a monumentally redundant exercise, since that voice, in all its rich idiosyncrasy, has long since left the building. This interdependence of form and content means that a poem can no more be translated than a piece of music. Certainly all a poet has to do is remind him or herself of the lines in which they take the most pride, and consider the minute nuances of sound and associations of meaning upon which that satisfaction rests, to realise they could not possibly find even their roughest equivalents in another tongue; a word in one language has valencies which in another will be entirely different. A poem derives much of its depth and complexity by developing the relationships between the vast entourage of semantic, acoustic and etymological friends, ghosts and ancestors that one word introduces to another. (In literal translation, the words often end up introducing one set of complete strangers to another; hence the result is usually just metred or unmetred prose – this kind of approach tends to limit its deviations from the original to the minimum number required to achieve a syntactic naturalism in the new language.) The non-poetry-writing reader is often possessed by the (perhaps necessary) illusion that the truth of a poem resides in its meaning, and that meaning can be carried into another language by an operation, that of simple transliteration; and that therefore what they read, when they read a translation, is more or less the original poem itself. This is very far from the truth. Literal translation can be useful in providing us with a black-and-white snapshot of the original, but a *version* – however subjectively – seeks to restore a light and colour and perspective. It does this by interpolating a process instead of an operation, and only a process can supply a poet with the time – from which proceeds the felicity, the kindness of strangers, and all luck one encounters on the road – that a real poem needs to be written. To reiterate: the only defensible fidelity is to the entirely subjective quality of 'spirit' or 'vision', rather than to literal meaning; though one can perhaps be truer, or at least not unfaithful, to the wider argument of a poem, and its images. But I can't believe that one should ever be true to a poet, least of all to the illusion of the 'great poet'; every decision would be infected by that sentimentality.

Machado's Spanish isn't English, and for that reason these poems are something like piano transcriptions of guitar music. The bare octaves and fifths that Machado plays can find no equivalent resonance in the great contraption, no matter how loudly we strike them. The only thing we can do is work in a little more chromaticism, a little directed emotional reading, in the hope that, occasionally, a *description* of a gravitas or an awe can stand for its unmediated sounding. To extend the analogy: the same note on the guitar can be played, with different resulting timbres, on several different strings, and to repeat 'alma' or 'camino' with Machado's frequency would simply sound disingenuous in a language with enough words, it seems at times, for everything to have a word to itself – as every note on the piano has a key to itself. There are no real synonyms, of course, so words are inevitably transposed into different registers; however, the alternative would have produced an unforgivable oversimplification, an emblem of simplicity rather than a simplicity itself.

The plan, in selecting from Machado's work, was to take

a leisurely stroll down the *via negativa*; with Machado as guide, a less bleak route than the brochures describe. The occasional outbreak of negative theology (not to be confused with negative faith) in the written word is characterised by a certain snowblindness, in that it plays – in a way that can be dangerous for the constitution of the poet, and dangerously boring for the reader – far closer to the annihilating light than other poetries. Brilliantly characterised by writers like W. S. Graham and Edmond Jabès, and caricatured by these very same writers at their worst, its literature is in a sense *dechromatised*, since it deals with the operation and transformation of light *within* the prism of poetic transformation, rather than how it bursts out on the further side – the side of mundane and quotidian diffraction, where all the stories, the details and the differences are. In the absence of any colour, then, darkness must be imported to give us something to talk about. The metaphor of the prism might help to explain the occasional intrusion of the discussion of the processes of art itself, which no doubt some will call 'postmodern'. (This self-reflexion, i.e. writing becoming aware of itself as writing, is a perennial and inevitable consequence of the serious play of the human imagination; 'postmodernism' is a literary tendency distinguished only by a self-conscious focus on this operation to the exclusion of others, and is thus, in its wilful exaggerations, a romantic one.) This is to misread and diminish Machado; he writes of writing only to deny his part in it, a double paradox – as if Escher's hands held erasers, not pens.

Finally, Machado's singerless song offers us the chance to make a quiet return to a poetry, if not of moral exhortation, then one of moral instruction; a function contemporary poetry seems to have forgotten it ever performed, it having been ceded – as if it were the last vestiges of an unhealthy didacticism – to religion and politics; but whose absence may well account for poetry's present irrelevance to the lives of many readers. These readers clearly have expectations of poetry which are not met by the work of most contemporary poets. I personally found them richly satisfied in reading Antonio Machado, and this book is a small attempt to communicate that.

One of the best things about this job is having so many dead friends you can talk to, and I should acknowledge here the tutelary voices of Machado's own mentor Miguel de Unamuno, and my own hand in the dark, Emil Cioran. Because of the integrity and self-delighted purity of his enterprise, Alan Trueblood's solid literal translations have more poetry in them than most poems, and I apologise to him for those two or three occasions where I have, without acknowledgement, stolen lines of his because they seemed pretty much unimprovable. Thanks are also due to the many friends who offered advice and encouragement.